NEW ORLEANS PELICANS

CONNOR STRATTON

WWW.APEXEDITIONS.COM

Apex is distributed by North Star Editions:
sales@northstareditions.com | 888-417-0195

Produced for Apex by Red Line Editorial.

Photographs ©: Tony Gutierrez/AP Images, cover, 1; Christian Petersen/Getty Images Sport/Getty Images, 4–5, 38–39; Jeremy Chen/Getty Images Sport/Getty Images, 6–7; Chris Graythen/Getty Images Sport/Getty Images, 8–9, 12–13, 26–27; Brian Bahr/Getty Images Sport/Getty Images, 10–11; Ronald Martinez/Getty Images Sport/Getty Images, 14–15; Ezra Shaw/Getty Images Sport/Getty Images, 16–17, 20–21; Ty Russell/AP Images, 19, 57; Otto Greule Jr./Getty Images Sport/Getty Images, 22–23; Elsa/Getty Images Sport/Getty Images, 24–25; Thearon W. Henderson/Getty Images Sport/Getty Images, 28–29, 30–31; Stacy Revere/Getty Images Sport/Getty Images, 32–33; Derick Hingle/AP Images, 34–35, 58–59; Jonathan Bachman/Getty Images Sport/Getty Images, 37, 44–45, 47; Jonathan Ferrey/Getty Images Sport/Getty Images, 40–41; Vaughn Ridley/Getty Images Sport/Getty Images, 42–43; iStockphoto, 48–49; Derick E. Hingle/Getty Images Sport/Getty Images, 50–51; Focus On Sport/Getty Images, 52–53; Sean Gardner/Getty Images Sport/Getty Images, 54–55

Library of Congress Control Number: 2025943703

ISBN
979-8-89250-911-4 (hardcover)
979-8-89250-942-8 (paperback)
979-8-89824-018-9 (ebook pdf)
979-8-89250-973-2 (hosted ebook)

Printed in the United States of America
Mankato, MN
012026

NOTE TO PARENTS AND EDUCATORS

Apex books are designed to build literacy skills in striving readers. Exciting, high-interest content attracts and holds readers' attention. The text is carefully leveled to allow students to achieve success quickly.

TABLE OF CONTENTS

CHAPTER 1

FIRST TRIPLE-DOUBLE

The New Orleans Pelicans had a small lead in the fourth quarter. Then Zion Williamson got the ball. The Pelicans forward slammed it through the hoop. The backboard shook after his huge dunk.

The New Orleans Pelicans played the Phoenix Suns on February 27, 2025.

Later, Williamson dished the ball across the court. His teammate sank a three-pointer. Williamson got the assist. With less than two minutes left, Williamson grabbed his 10th rebound. That earned him the first triple-double of his career. His play helped the Pelicans defeat the Phoenix Suns.

GETTING EVEN BETTER

Injuries limited Zion Williamson in the 2024–25 season. But when he was healthy, he played better than ever. Williamson's defensive skills improved. He was a stronger playmaker, too.

Zion Williamson recorded 27 points, 10 rebounds, and 11 assists in his first career triple-double.

CHAPTER 2

EARLY HISTORY

The New Orleans Pelicans have an unusual history. They began as the Charlotte Hornets. The Hornets moved to New Orleans for the 2002–03 season. At first, the National Basketball Association (NBA) considered it the same team in a new city. But now, the league considers it the start of a new team.

The Hornets reached the playoffs in their first two seasons after moving to New Orleans.

In his first NBA season, Chris Paul (3) averaged 16.1 points, 5.1 rebounds, and 7.8 assists per game.

The New Orleans Hornets played well for two seasons. However, the success didn't last. The Hornets lost a lot of games in 2004–05. The rough season had one benefit, though. The Hornets got the fourth pick in the draft. They selected point guard Chris Paul.

FIRST GAME ROUT

In the Hornets' first game in New Orleans, they played the Utah Jazz. The Jazz had played in New Orleans from 1974 to 1979. The Hornets won the game. They crushed the Jazz 100–75.

In August 2005, Hurricane Katrina hit New Orleans. The storm devastated the city. The area needed time to rebuild. So, the Hornets had to move for a while. The team ended up in Oklahoma City, Oklahoma. The Hornets played there for two seasons.

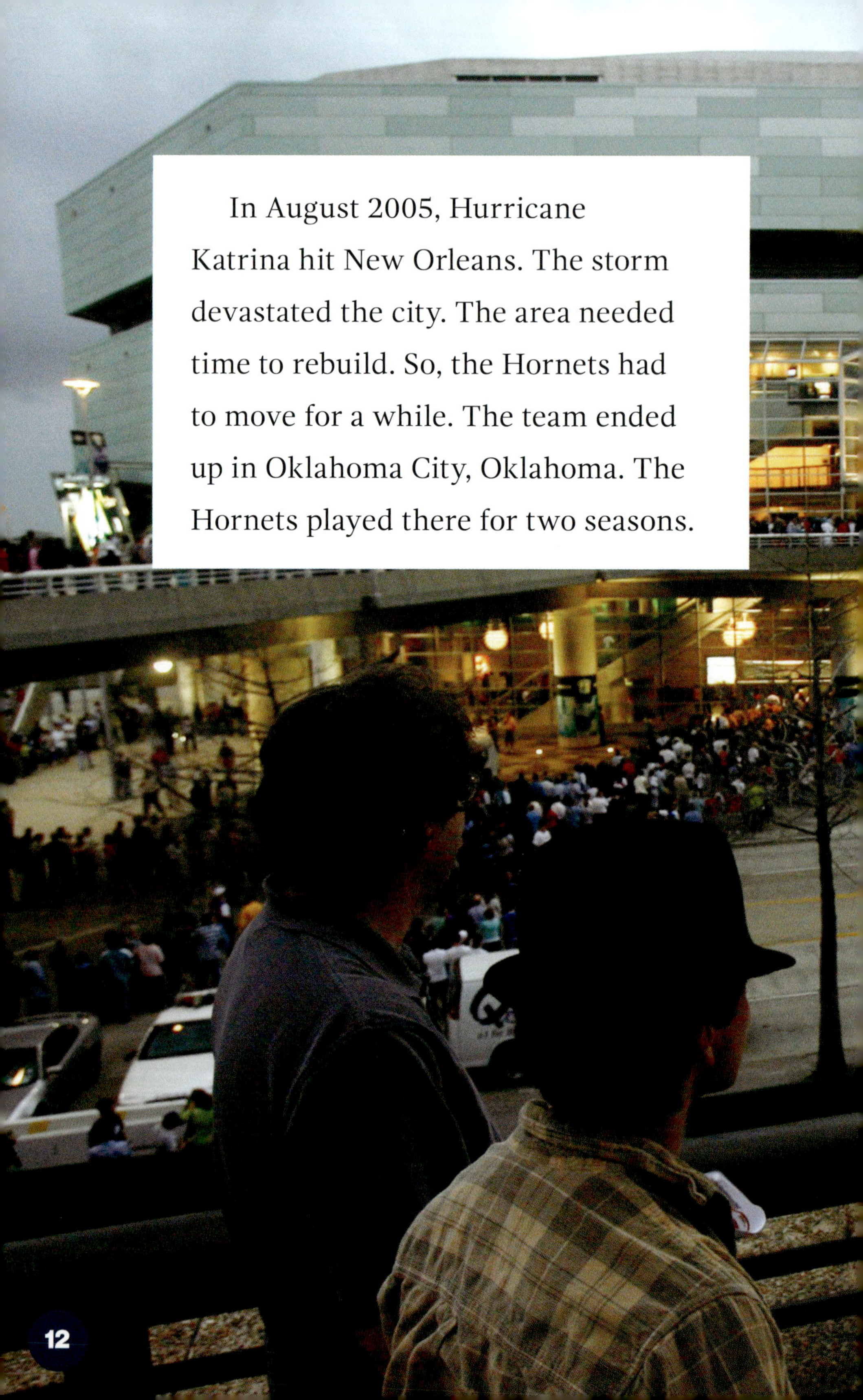

Local fans were excited to welcome the Hornets back to New Orleans.

BACK HOME

In the 2005–06 and 2006–07 seasons, the Hornets returned to New Orleans for a few games. The first game back was in March 2006. The city was still struggling. Many people from New Orleans were living elsewhere. But the game still sold out.

In the 2007–08 season, the Hornets resumed playing in New Orleans full time. The return home boosted their play. They went 56–26. That was the team's best season ever. But the Hornets fell in the second round of the playoffs.

MADE FOR TV

In 2009, Chris Paul hit an incredible fadeaway buzzer-beater. The basket won the game for New Orleans. The NBA featured the sweet shot in TV ads.

Chris Paul averaged 11.3 assists per game in the 2008 playoffs.

Anthony Davis made 51.6 percent of his shots during his rookie season.

New Orleans traded Paul in 2011. The team struggled without him. However, big changes came in 2012. A new owner bought the team that year. The team also received the first pick in the draft. New Orleans selected power forward Anthony Davis.

CHANGING OWNERS

In 2010, the Hornets' owner wanted to sell the team. But no one would buy it. At first, the NBA took over as owner. Then, in 2012, Tom Benson bought the Hornets. He also owned the New Orleans Saints football team. Benson didn't plan to move the basketball team. New Orleans fans felt relieved.

CHRIS PAUL

Chris Paul was a master point guard. He led the Hornets offense with his vision and intelligence. Paul often spotted open teammates. Then he passed them the ball for easy shots. If a teammate wasn't open, Paul could score from nearly anywhere.

Paul was a great defender, too. He led the league in steals three times in New Orleans. Those turnovers made for easy buckets on the other end. As of 2025, Paul remained the team's all-time leader in steals and assists.

CHRIS PAUL WON THE ROOKIE OF THE YEAR AWARD IN THE 2005–06 SEASON.

OKC

CHAPTER 3

LEGENDS

When the Hornets moved from Charlotte to New Orleans, P. J. Brown moved with them. He played tough offense and defense. Brown was a great rebounder, too. He averaged 8.5 per game with New Orleans.

P. J. Brown averaged 10.3 points per game with New Orleans.

Jamal Mashburn was New Orleans's first All-Star. The forward scored from all over the court. Injuries cut his career short. But some of Mashburn's best years came with the Hornets.

EARLY STAR

Baron Davis was a key piece of New Orleans's early years. His best season came in 2003–04. Davis led the team in scoring. He also nabbed 2.4 steals per game. That led the NBA.

Jamal Mashburn led the Hornets in total points and scoring in the team's first season in New Orleans.

The Hornets picked David West in the 2003 draft. The power forward was tough. His physical play helped him score in the paint. It also created space to score from midrange. West formed an amazing duo with Chris Paul. The pair destroyed defenses with their pick-and-roll.

As of 2025, David West was still second all-time in total points for New Orleans.

In the 2007–08 season, New Orleans was stacked with talent. The team built their defense around Tyson Chandler. The towering center made an impact on offense, too. Chandler led the league in offensive rebounds that season.

SHARPSHOOTER

Peja Stojaković joined New Orleans in 2006. He was deadly from long range. During the 2007–08 season, he averaged 3.0 three-pointers per game. That was the most in the NBA.

Tyson Chandler (left) averaged 4.4 offensive rebounds per game in the 2007–08 season.

CHAPTER 4

RECENT HISTORY

For the 2013–2014 season, the Hornets changed their name. The team's owner wanted a name that connected to New Orleans. He decided on the Pelicans. That is the state bird of Louisiana. In 2014, Charlotte's new NBA team took back the Hornets name.

New Orleans had a losing record in the team's first season as the Pelicans.

Anthony Davis brought new energy to New Orleans. In the early 2010s, the team steadily improved. By the 2014–15 season, the Pelicans were back in the playoffs.

DROPPING 59

In a February 2016 game, Anthony Davis had an incredible day. He scored a career-high 59 points. And he grabbed 20 rebounds. As of 2024–25, his point total remained a team record.

Anthony Davis averaged three blocks per game in the 2015 playoffs.

Injuries set the Pelicans back in the 2015–16 season. They struggled the next season, too. But New Orleans bounced back in 2017–18. Davis led the Pelicans to their first playoff series win in 10 years.

UNDERDOG WINNERS

The Pelicans faced the Portland Trail Blazers in the 2018 playoffs. A group of sports experts predicted the winner. All 22 people picked Portland. But the Pelicans shocked them all. They swept the Trail Blazers in four games.

Rajon Rondo averaged 12.2 assists per game in the 2018 playoffs.

Zion Williamson averaged 24.7 points per game in his first five seasons with New Orleans.

Davis left New Orleans after the 2018–19 season. But the Pelicans received another top draft pick. They selected Zion Williamson. New Orleans built an exciting group around the young star. In 2024, the Pelicans reached the playoffs for the second time in three years.

LUCKY NO. 1

The Pelicans struggled in the 2018–19 season. But several other teams played worse. So, those teams had higher chances of winning the draft lottery. The lottery winner gets the first pick. The Pelicans had only a small chance. But luck turned their way. New Orleans got the top pick.

PLAYER SPOTLIGHT

ANTHONY DAVIS

Anthony Davis stood six feet, ten inches (208 cm) tall. He had a wingspan of seven feet, six inches (229 cm). His size and physical play helped him dominate. Davis grabbed rebound after rebound. On offense, he dazzled fans with his monster dunks. And on defense, few were better at blocking shots. Davis led the NBA in blocks three times.

Davis also earned All-Star honors six times in seven seasons with New Orleans. He became the team's leader in scoring, rebounds, and blocks.

ANTHONY DAVIS MADE THE ALL-DEFENSIVE FIRST TEAM IN THE 2017–18 SEASON.

ZATARAINS
NEW ORLEANS
23

Eric Gordon averaged 15.3 points per game over five seasons with New Orleans.

CHAPTER 5

MODERN STARS

Eric Gordon joined New Orleans in 2011. He delivered much-needed scoring to the team. Ryan Anderson joined the next season. The smooth shooter averaged 16.1 points per game during his time with the Pelicans.

Jrue Holiday joined New Orleans in 2013. The point guard was an excellent two-way player. Holiday made the All-Defensive first team in 2017–18. He also shined during the Pelicans' 2018 playoff run.

BRIEF BUT BRIGHT

DeMarcus Cousins played less than two seasons with the Pelicans. He struggled with injuries during his time in New Orleans. But he played a huge role in 2017–18. The center averaged 25.2 points per game that season.

In the 2018 playoffs, Jrue Holiday averaged 23.7 points, 5.7 rebounds, and 6.3 assists per game.

Brandon Ingram made his first All-Star Game in his first season with New Orleans.

In 2019, the Pelicans started building around Zion Williamson. New Orleans traded for Brandon Ingram. The move paid off right away. The power forward averaged 23 points per game over six seasons.

DRAFT SUCCESS

New Orleans had a great draft in 2021. The Pelicans traded for the 17th pick. They used it on Trey Murphy III. Murphy became one of the team's top scorers. The Pelicans also selected Herbert Jones in the second round. By 2023, Jones was one of the NBA's top defenders.

In 2022, the Pelicans picked up CJ McCollum. The guard provided the young team with key experience. McCollum spent several seasons in New Orleans. During that time, he became the Pelicans' leading three-point shooter.

PROMISING TRADE

The Pelicans traded for Dejounte Murray in 2024. The point guard cut through defenses. He found open teammates left and right. And his steals created easy buckets on offense.

CJ McCollum made 3.1 three-pointers per game with New Orleans.

PLAYER SPOTLIGHT

ZION WILLIAMSON

Zion Williamson was shorter than many power forwards. But he weighed more than 280 pounds (127 kg). Thanks to his size, Williamson scored most of his points in the paint. He overpowered defenders near the basket.

Williamson had an incredible scoring ability. He scored 2,000 points in just 79 games. That was the fastest since NBA legend Michael Jordan. Williamson made the All-Star team twice in his first few seasons with the Pelicans.

IN THE 2022–23 SEASON, ZION WILLIAMSON MADE 60.8 PERCENT OF HIS SHOTS.

NEW ORLEANS
1
ibotta
Wilson

CHAPTER 6

TEAM TRIVIA

The Pelicans' colors are blue, red, and gold. That matches New Orleans's flag. The team's logo features a "bird-de-lis." It is a pelican in the shape of a fleur-de-lis. This flower is a symbol of New Orleans.

The fleur-de-lis is connected to France. It highlights New Orleans's French roots.

The Pelicans have played in the same arena since 2002. The venue has hosted many other major events. That includes the NBA All-Star Game. The event happened in New Orleans in 2008, 2014, and 2017.

AFTER KATRINA

The Pelicans' arena survived Hurricane Katrina. It reopened less than a month after the storm. However, the surrounding area remained damaged. The team couldn't return home for years.

The team's arena can hold nearly 17,000 fans for Pelicans games.

"Pistol" Pete Maravich played for the New Orleans Jazz in the 1970s. The Hall of Famer led the league in scoring in 1976–77. At the Hornets' first game in New Orleans, the team retired Maravich's jersey. No player could wear No. 7.

BASKETBALL CITY

New Orleans has been home to several basketball teams over the years. The Hurricanes played there in 1947. Then came the Buccaneers in 1967. The Buccaneers were part of the American Basketball Association (ABA). The Jazz were the first NBA team in New Orleans. They moved to Utah in 1979.

Pete Maravich's jersey was retired on October 30, 2011.

Pierre T. Pelican became the mascot in 2013. King Cake Baby joined a year later.

When the Hornets became the Pelicans, the team got a new mascot. His name is Pierre T. Pelican. The mascot features a bright yellow beak. He pumps up the crowd during games.

KING CAKE BABY

The Pelicans have a bonus mascot. King Cake Baby comes out during Mardi Gras. He wears only a diaper, a bib, and a crown. The city loves the strange mascot. It even inspired movie characters.

TEAM RECORDS

All-Time Points: 11,059
Anthony Davis (2012–19)

All-Time Assists: 4,228
Chris Paul (2005–11)

All-Time Rebounds: 4,906
Anthony Davis (2012–19)

All-Time Steals: 1,010
Chris Paul (2005–11)

All-Time Blocks: 1,121
Anthony Davis (2012–19)

All-Time Three-Pointers: 692
CJ McCollum (2021–25)

All-Time Triple-Doubles: 11
Chris Paul (2005–11)

All-Time Games Played: 530
David West (2003–11)

All-Time Coaching Wins: 203
Byron Scott (2004–10)

All-Time Points Per Game: 24.7
Zion Williamson (2019–)

All statistics are accurate through the 2024–25 season.

HORNETS
3
NBA

TIMELINE

2002

The Charlotte Hornets move to New Orleans, and P. J. Brown leads them to the playoffs in their first two seasons.

2005

New Orleans drafts Chris Paul, who becomes the face of the team.

2005

In August, Hurricane Katrina hits Louisiana. The Hornets move to Oklahoma City.

2007

The Hornets return to New Orleans full time. They win a team-record 56 games and reach the conference semifinals in the 2008 playoffs.

2010

The NBA buys the Hornets before finding a new owner in 2012.

2012

New Orleans selects Anthony Davis with the first pick in the draft.

2013

The Hornets change their name to the Pelicans.

2018

Anthony Davis leads the Pelicans to their first conference semifinals in 10 years.

2019

The Pelicans win the draft lottery to earn the top pick. They select Zion Williamson.

2024

The Pelicans make the playoffs for the second time in three seasons.

COMPREHENSION QUESTIONS

Write your answers on a separate piece of paper.

1. Write a paragraph that explains the main ideas of Chapter 5.
2. Who do you think was the greatest player in Pelicans history? Why?
3. When did the Hornets change their name to the Pelicans?
   - **A.** 2002
   - **B.** 2013
   - **C.** 2019
4. Why did the Pelicans start building their team around Zion Williamson in 2019?
   - **A.** The Pelicans wanted to get players who worked well with their star.
   - **B.** The Pelicans wanted older players who would learn from Williamson.
   - **C.** The Pelicans planned to trade Williamson the next season.

5. What does **dominate** mean in this book?

His size and physical play helped him **dominate**. *Davis grabbed rebound after rebound. On offense, he dazzled fans with his monster dunks. And on defense, few were better at blocking shots.*

A. make lots of foolish mistakes
B. play much better than others
C. take shots from far away

6. What does **retired** mean in this book?

The Hall of Famer led the league in scoring in 1976–77. At the Hornets' first game in New Orleans, the team **retired** *Maravich's jersey. No player could wear No. 7.*

A. joined a team that had a long history of winning games
B. ended a career after playing in a league for many seasons
C. honored a player by making his number off-limits

Answer key on page 64.

GLOSSARY

assist
A pass that leads directly to a basket.

buzzer-beater
A shot made with no time left on the game clock.

draft
A system that lets teams select new players coming into the league.

lottery
A system that picks a winner at random.

mascot
A figure that is the symbol of a sports team.

paint
The area between the basket and the free-throw line.

pick-and-roll
A play when someone blocks a defender and then moves to receive a pass.

playoffs
A set of games played after the regular season to decide which team is the champion.

rookie
An athlete in his or her first year as a professional player.

triple-double
A game in which a player records 10 or more of three different stats.

two-way
Excelling on both offense and defense.

TO LEARN MORE

BOOKS

Giedd, Steph. *New Orleans Pelicans All-Time Greats*. Press Box Books, 2024.

Glave, Tom. *New Orleans Pelicans*. Abdo Publishing, 2023.

Whiting, Jim. *The Story of the New Orleans Pelicans*. Creative Education, 2023.

ONLINE RESOURCES

Visit **www.apexeditions.com** to find links and resources related to this title.

ABOUT THE AUTHOR

Connor Stratton writes and edits nonfiction children's books. He lives in Minnesota.

INDEX

ANSWER KEY:

1. Answers will vary; 2. Answers will vary; 3. B; 4. A; 5. B; 6. C